THE UNSEEN
BEATLES

THE UNSEEN BEATLES

PHOTOGRAPHS BY BOB WHITAKER

ACCOMPANYING TEXT BY MARTIN HARRISON

CollinsPublishersSanFrancisco

A Division of HarperCollins*Publishers*

First published in the United States of America in 1991 by
CollinsPublishersSanFrancisco

First published in 1991 by Conran Octopus Limited

Editorial director: Anne Furniss
Design: Barney Wan
Production: Julia Golding

Library of Congress Cataloging-in-Publication Data
Whitaker, Bob.
The unseen Beatles/photographs by Bob Whitaker;
accompanying text by Martin Harrison.
        p.   cm.
''First published 1991 by Conran Octopus Limited . . . London''—
T.p. verso.
        ISBN 0-00-215953-8

1. Beatles—Pictorial works.   2. Rock musicians—England–
–Pictorial works.   I. Harrison, Martin, 1945–   . II. Title.

ML421.B4W5   1991
782.42166'092'2—dc20   91-19282
                                        CIP
                                        MN

Printed and bound in Hong Kong; first printing 1991

10 9 8 7 6 5 4 3 2 1

ACKNOWLEDGMENTS

I would like to pay particular tribute and thanks to Robert Hershkowitz for his endless support and suggestions regarding my collection of negatives and prints which survived in my damp barns and chicken sheds during the years that my wife and I have spent farming and raising our three children. Thanks and much love to my wife Susan for her support and understanding during all our moves from farm to farm, and her wisdom in raising three very stable children. Susan is a tower of strength, love and kindness.

To Martin Sharp, whose clarity of thought never failed to make me laugh to my very sinews, and to all of my friends in Australia with whom I spent such a happy youth.

To Alan Bull, Lawrence Bull, and a fine photographer Trevor Legate at Taurus Photographic in Crawley for their advice and my use of their facilities.

Thanks to the magnificent ladies who run Conran Octopus for their encouragement, advice, and endless time: especially Anne Furniss for her persistence of motivation without which this project would still languish in the chicken shed.

Barney Wan, who has been a great friend since I arrived back in this country in 1964, has patiently waited to lay out this book for years. Thank you Barney for your careful thoughts and masterly art direction.

Bob Whitaker.

INTRODUCTION

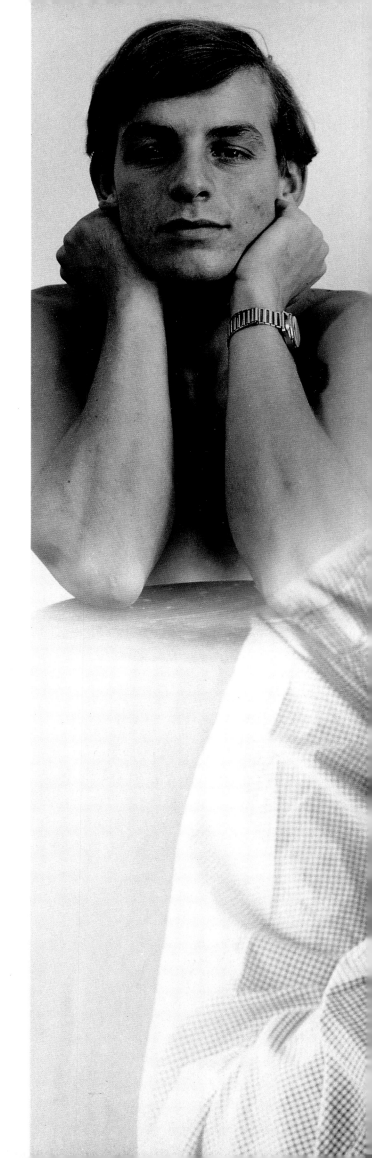

The photographs in this book are the result of
a fortuitous meeting with Brian Epstein, the
Beatles' manager, during their tour of Australia in 1964.

At the time I was 23 years old and coping
with the pleasures of running my own photographic studio in Melbourne. Fashion, adver-
tising and magazine editorials were my main
source of income. Like most people of my age
in Australia I was mad keen on the Beatles, but
never thought for a moment that I might
photograph them. When the Beatles arrived
in Melbourne, a journalist friend of mine
telephoned to say he had been commissioned to interview Brian Epstein, and
would I come along to take photographs.

We duly arrived at the Southern Cross
Hotel, to be confronted by a huge crowd in
the street, later estimated to have been a
quarter of a million people. The hotel lobby
was pandemonium as journalists and photographers battled with one another in their
attempts to get interviews with the Beatles.
Since ours was prearranged we were swiftly
escorted to the lifts and up to Mr Epstein's
suite, to the amazement of the other frustrated
members of the media.

We were shown into the guest lounge of a
very grand suite to await him. Outside, many
floors below, we could hear the constant
chanting of the crowd, occasionally punc-
tuated by a roar and cheers as someone,
possibly a Beatle but perhaps some other
unsuspecting hotel guest, appeared at a

Dual portrait: Brian Epstein and Bob Whitaker,
Melbourne, June 1964.

6

window. The youth of Australia craved culture, and the Beatles were the biggest act to hit the place.

Brian Epstein entered and the interview began. He was immaculately dressed: well-pressed trousers, gingham shirt, smart shoes, silk socks, an expensive watch and a gold bracelet. A bit of a peacock I thought, as I cautiously proceeded to take some pictures. Rather formal at first, he gradually relaxed, and at the end of the interview asked me to let him see the photographs before he left Melbourne.

Back in my darkroom I made a contact sheet and some prints for the newspaper. I studied the photographs and realized that, although they were a good likeness, they did not convey my feelings as I took them. Brian had shown that he had a great sense of humour and I decided he should have something better as a souvenir of Australia.

At the time I was trying to get my thoughts down on photographic paper in the form of multiple exposures. These were made not in the camera but at the enlarging stage in the darkroom. Using some peacock feathers and two of the shots I had taken of Brian I made a couple of these images: portraits of Brian with peacock feathers around his head. At once he was revealed the way I had seen him – a peacock, an emperor. Then I wondered how I should sign my photographs. It could be easily done with a rubber stamp, but I wanted something more personal. I found some negatives of myself in the file, exposed them either side of Brian's portrait, and there it was, a signature with a difference.

I made an appointment to hand over my photographs to Brian at the hotel. Greeted by the same mad crowds, I called Brian on the in-house telephone and we agreed to meet in the lobby. As soon as he stepped out of the lift he was accosted by the crowd, but I managed to struggle through and hand him my envelope. He opened it there and then and three large prints slid onto the floor in full view of the assembled masses. Brian turned scarlet, retrieved the photographs, laughed and said he would call me later when he had found a chance to look properly at them.

Amazingly, he was as good as his word. He rang later that day and asked if he could visit my studio to see more of my work. He loved the multiple exposures and the way I had put across my ideas. On the spot he made me an incredible offer. He would like me to come to the U.K., where he would manage me as a photographer and I would also become his 'artistic adviser'. What a fantastic opportunity!

AUSTRALIA

Bob Whitaker, self portrait,
Melbourne, December 1963.

Though he was born and raised in England, Bob's father and grandfather were Australian and he went to Melbourne in 1961, originally to supervise the installation of a colour-film processing plant, but by the time he arrived the project had been abandoned. Instead he found employment as a film editor with the television channel ABV2.

It was at ABV2 that he met Nigel Buesst. "We started to go to all of the film festivals. European new-wave cinema, and the work of directors like Eisenstein, provided one of my most formative visual influences." He and Buesst built a darkroom together, and Bob began photographing events such as jazz conventions as well as his new-found group of friends. Significantly, Buesst's parents owned an important collection of contemporary Australian art. The 1959 *Antipodean* exhibition had focused attention on Australian artists, who were asserting their origina-

lity on a world stage. Far from finding himself in a cultural backwater, Bob was thrust into a buoyant and stimulating milieu.

"Suddenly my spare time was taken up discussing ideas about art and philosophy. I became friendly with the painter Mirka Mora and her husband, George; these conversations would continue at George's Melbourne restaurant, the Balzac, and at regular Friday night meetings at the house of the architect Peter Burns." Bob soon got to know many of the leading painters in this circle, Don Laycock, Arthur Boyd, Charles Blackman, Albert Tucker, and John Perceval.

Concurrently with this leap into new territories, Bob was pushing along his photography. He left his television job to work alongside an established Melbourne photographer, Lloyd Buchanan, but soon progressed to the point where he was able to open his own studio. A few doors away were

Olivia Newton-John, Melbourne, April 1963.

George and Mirka Mora, Melbourne, June 1963.

the offices of Australian *Vogue*, and the magazine quickly helped to launch his career as a fashion photographer.

"But I soon became bored with fashion," recalls Bob, "it always seemed diluted – I was more interested in photography as a medium for personal expression." Reacting against his commercial work, he photographed Rona Goldsmith, one of his favourite fashion models, together with her husband and baby. "Her home life appeared surprisingly mundane. It seemed that most women — however pretty – were destined to become enslaved by domesticity. So I posed Rona's sister, the fourteen-year-old Olivia Newton-John, hung up on a washing line carrying a packet of soap powder to symbolize the grim future in prospect."

At the same time Bob began to experiment in the darkroom, combining images from more than one negative on the same sheet of photographic paper. He also adapted the 'rayogram' technique of Surrealist painter/ photographer Man Ray, combining it with straight photography. This involved laying actual objects on the print surface before exposing it to light – a method he later used to add the peacock feathers to his portrait of Brian Epstein.

Apart from the Australian artists he got to know, it was the Dadaists and Surrealists who provided much of Bob's inspiration. Before he left England he had cut up a Salvador Dali book and sent the collaged results to Dali himself. "He sent a charming reply, inviting me to Spain, an offer I was able to take up eight years later when I photographed him over a long period of time in Spain, France and the U.S."

As Bob's social sphere expanded he encountered many individuals who later played a part in his career. They included art historian Robert Hughes (together they reported on the devastation wrought by the Florence floods), cartoonist Martin Sharp, and journalist and poet Adrian Rawlins. In June 1964, Rawlins, described by Bob as "an Antipodean Ginsberg", was commissioned by the *Jewish News* to interview Brian Epstein. He asked Bob to take the photographs. It was an experience that changed the course of his life.

Paul with boomerang, Melbourne, June 1964.

BACK IN THE U.K.

John between shooting takes of the film *Help*,
Cliveden, Buckinghamshire, May 1965.

Brian Epstein's invitation to join his empire seemed like an offer Bob could not refuse, but at first he hesitated. He was turning his back not only on his first commercial success but also on the growing recognition for his experimental photographs; when the Beatles arrived in Australia his work was included in *Photo-Vision*, a group show at Melbourne's Museum of Modern Art. He asked for time to consider the move. "But the Beatles' concert had made a major impact on me," Bob later said, "and after three months I finally took the plunge."

The timing was perfect. Although he had briefly met the Beatles in Melbourne, back in the U.K. he got to know them better in the marginally less pressured atmosphere of a tour on their home ground. Gaining their confidence was essential. Eventually it would mean Bob could rely on their collaboration in some of the most original and unusual photographs ever taken of the group.

"Brian Epstein was one of the most honourable people I have ever met," says Bob. He was engaged as an independent artist, whose career Epstein intended to direct. This meant that Bob was allowed unrestricted creative freedom in his photography.

The Beatles take a break from
touring, Scotland, October 1964.

The Beatles' limo enters Plymouth,
October 1964.

Fans outside Hammersmith Odeon, London, December 1964.

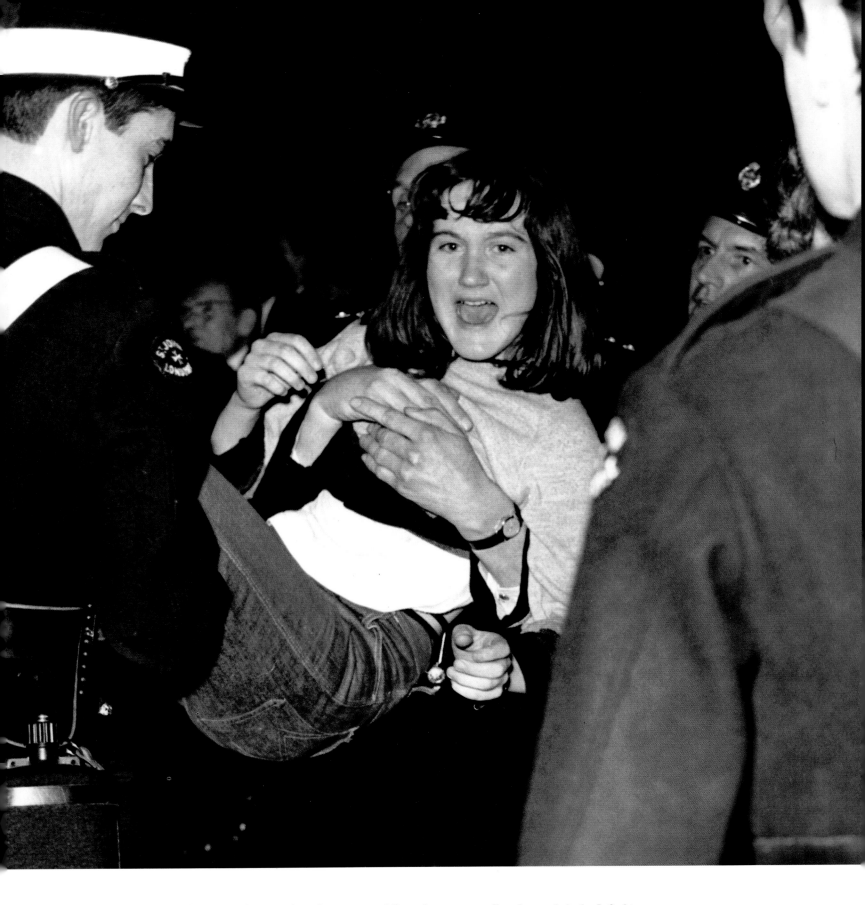

"*The exception to the rule. I never liked to use flash, which I felt imposed its own artificial atmosphere on events. Here there was no alternative – it was pitch black. On this occasion I thought flash would help to emphasize the flailing limbs of the fans struggling to see their heroes.*"

The Beatles were in Chiswick Park to film a television promotional film for their forthcoming single, *Paperback Writer*. In the afternoon children from the local grammar school were returning home and realized what was going on in the park. A crowd soon gathered, hoping for a glimpse of their heroes.

This dramatic photograph succeeds in epitomizing, in a single image, the glamour, fame and magnetism of the Beatles.

George and fans, Chiswick Park, London, May 1966.

"Somehow one schoolgirl got through the security net. You can imagine how thrilled she was. It was quite touching – the Beatles were so friendly towards her and behaved like perfect gentlemen."

Chiswick Park, London, May 1966.

"This was not posed – it was something which just happened before my camera. I simply moved in close and framed as tightly as I could, so that there was no requirement for cropping later. Except in the studio, I never asked the Beatles to pose for me."

George resting between takes, Chiswick Park, London, May 1966.

Following pages: Chiswick Park, London, May 1966.

At the E.M.I. recording
studios, London,
May 1966.
The photograph
was used on
the back cover
of *Revolver*.

Ringo had been hospitalized for the removal of his tonsils, and George was on holiday in the Bahamas, so rehearsals for the Beatles 1964/5 Christmas Shows in London started very late. "They were very good about having someone constantly there with a camera," comments Bob, "they never made me feel I was in the way." Back in the U.K., Bob had to develop his techniques for shooting in low-light situations, pushing film to its limit. The Donmar Hall presented an especially difficult task, being lit by only one 300 watt bulb way up in the ceiling. The results justify the technical struggle, retaining the mood as well as the immediacy of the occasion.

At rehearsal, Donmar Hall, Covent Garden, London, December 1964.

"This was taken on a half-frame camera — 72 shots on a roll — and the only illumination came from the Rolls-Royce's interior light. It's not surprising my photographs were sometimes considered unsuitable for reproduction in newspapers."

Ringo returning from Manchester, October 1964.

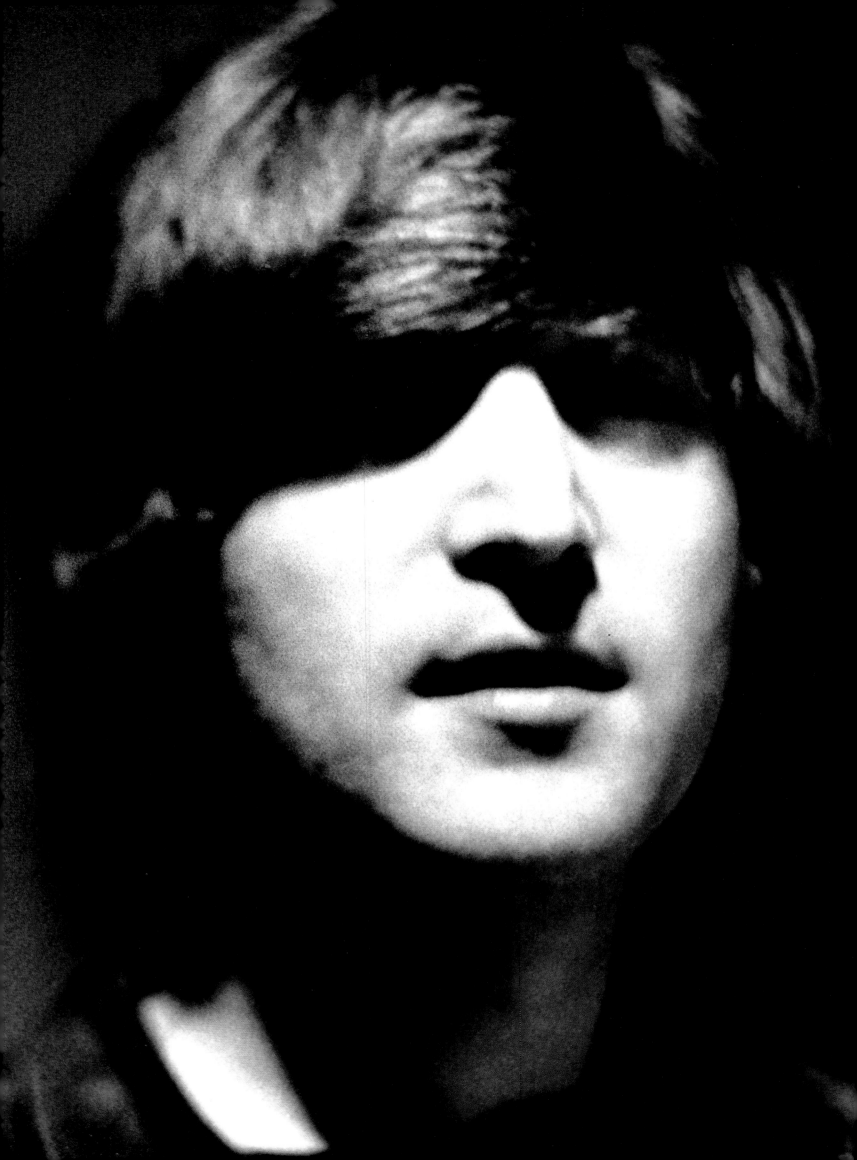

ON TOUR IN THE U.S.

Rushing for the helicopter, Pan Am building,
New York, August 1965.

The Beatles' concert at New York's Shea Stadium on August 15 1965 was watched by over 55,000 fans, which was, at that time, a world record attendance. Bob witnessed Beatlemania at its height.

"The journey to the Shea had to be organized like a military operation. We flew by helicopter from the top of the Pan Am building in Manhattan and transferred to an armoured Wells Fargo truck near the stadium. It had no windows, and the kids were hammering on the outside and rocking it; the noise was deafening, the screaming and screeching was really terrifying. At one stage we thought the truck was going to tip over and we were all going to get dragged out and torn to pieces."

Touring was incredibly demanding – a mixture of intense, hectic pressure on the one hand and abject boredom and interminable waiting on the other. Bob was fascinated by the contrast between onstage excitement and the frenzy of the fans, and behind-the-scenes preparation, relaxation, tiredness and tedium. His freedom of access to shoot wherever and whenever he wanted facilitated a perceptive record of these two extremes of life on tour.

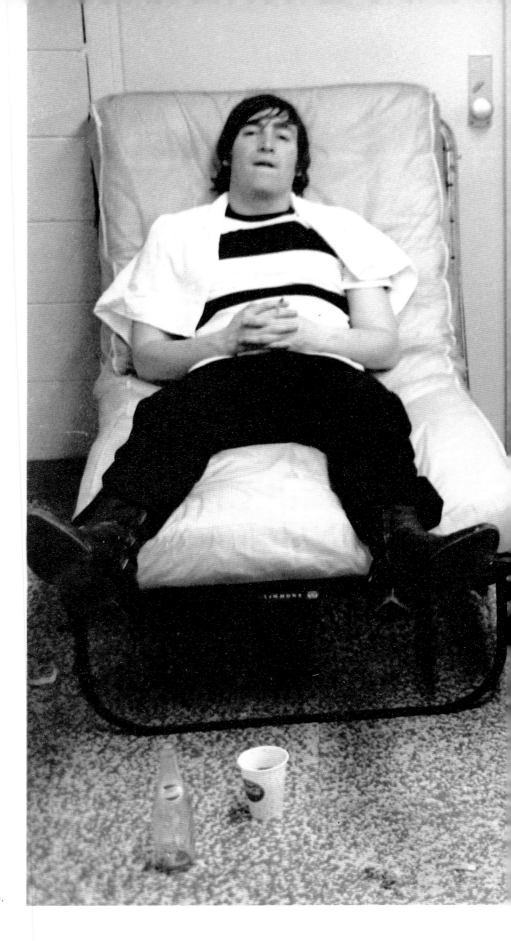

Before the concert, Toronto, August 1965.

Three tired and apprehensive Beatles waiting to go onstage at the Maple Leaf Gardens. Ringo had just announced to the press that he was having a go-karting track built at his house in England. After the Shea Stadium concert the group had interrupted their U.S. itinerary for this one-off concert in Canada.

In Atlanta Airport, waiting to fly to Houston, August 1965.

"The shedules were punishing. You hardly knew which city you were in. What I mostly remember about touring is being constantly ushered onto planes along with the Beatles and their supporting cast."

"At every stop there were people to greet, interviews, autographs to sign. And in every dressing room there would be piles of gifts the fans had left for the Beatles. Here a girl had presented a painting she had made for Ringo."

Ringo in the dressing room, Toronto, August 1965.

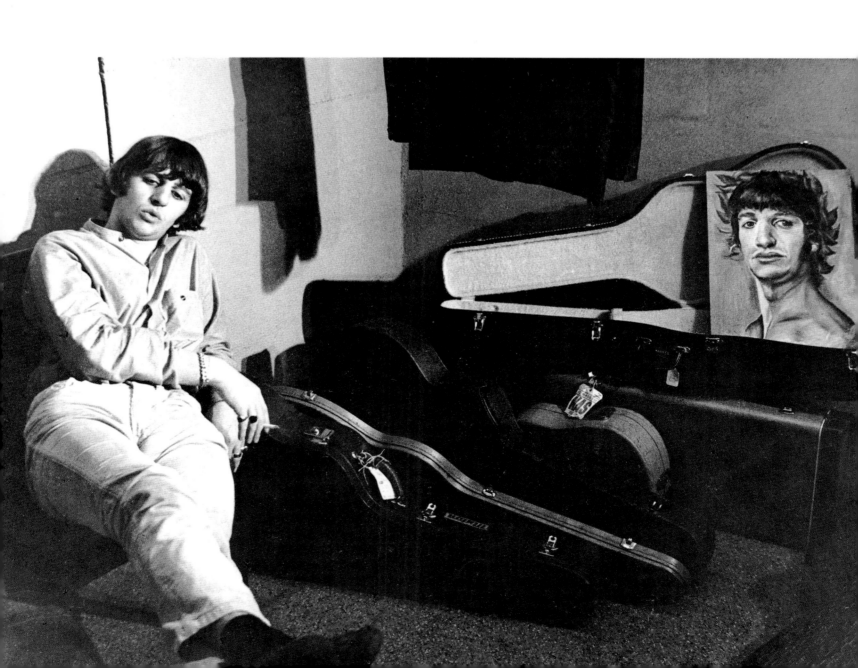

Ringo catches up with the Beatles' story, Houston, August 1965.

John relaxes after the concert, Chicago, August 1965.

Overleaf: "How do you brush your teeth, Beatles?" Answering questions at a press conference, August 1965.

WELCOME To
WDGY LAND

ON TOUR: GERMANY

Greeting the crowd, Munich, June 1966.

In June 1966 the Beatles returned for a short tour to the country where, at the Star Club in Hamburg, they had learned much of their craft at the beginning of the decade.

Bob joined the Beatles on their four-day visit, expecting to return to England after its completion. But after the final concert in Hamburg they invited him to accompany them on the second leg of the tour on to Tokyo. Ironically he seemed to have become an indispensable part of the team just before they stopped touring for good.

Again, his photographs record not only their actual performances but also allow us to share in the more private moments of the Beatles off-stage. Typical are his intriguing glimpses of Ringo at Munich: "Ringo was such an ardent wit. And he obviously enjoyed his clothes enormously; he never failed to amaze me with his suits."

John in the Bayerschoff Hotel, Munich, June 1966.

The Beatles' guitars were always carefully laid out on a table in the dressing room. Note the running order of songs for the concert marked on George's Epiphone guitar.

Ernst Mercke Halle, Hamburg, June 1966.

Following pages:

Crowd outside the Ernst Mercke Halle, Hamburg, June 1966.

Martin Sharp added the balloon caption later in the year. It refers to an actual incident Bob had related to him. Brian Epstein had left the hall at Hamburg by a side entrance, forgetting his stage pass. Trying to get back in before the concert he could not convince the security guards who he was. Finally he summoned up all his authority and managed to persuade a policeman to go inside the hall and check his credentials, getting back in just before the concert began.

Performing at the Circus-Krone-Bau, Munich, June 1966.

Last minute run-through, Munich, June 1966.

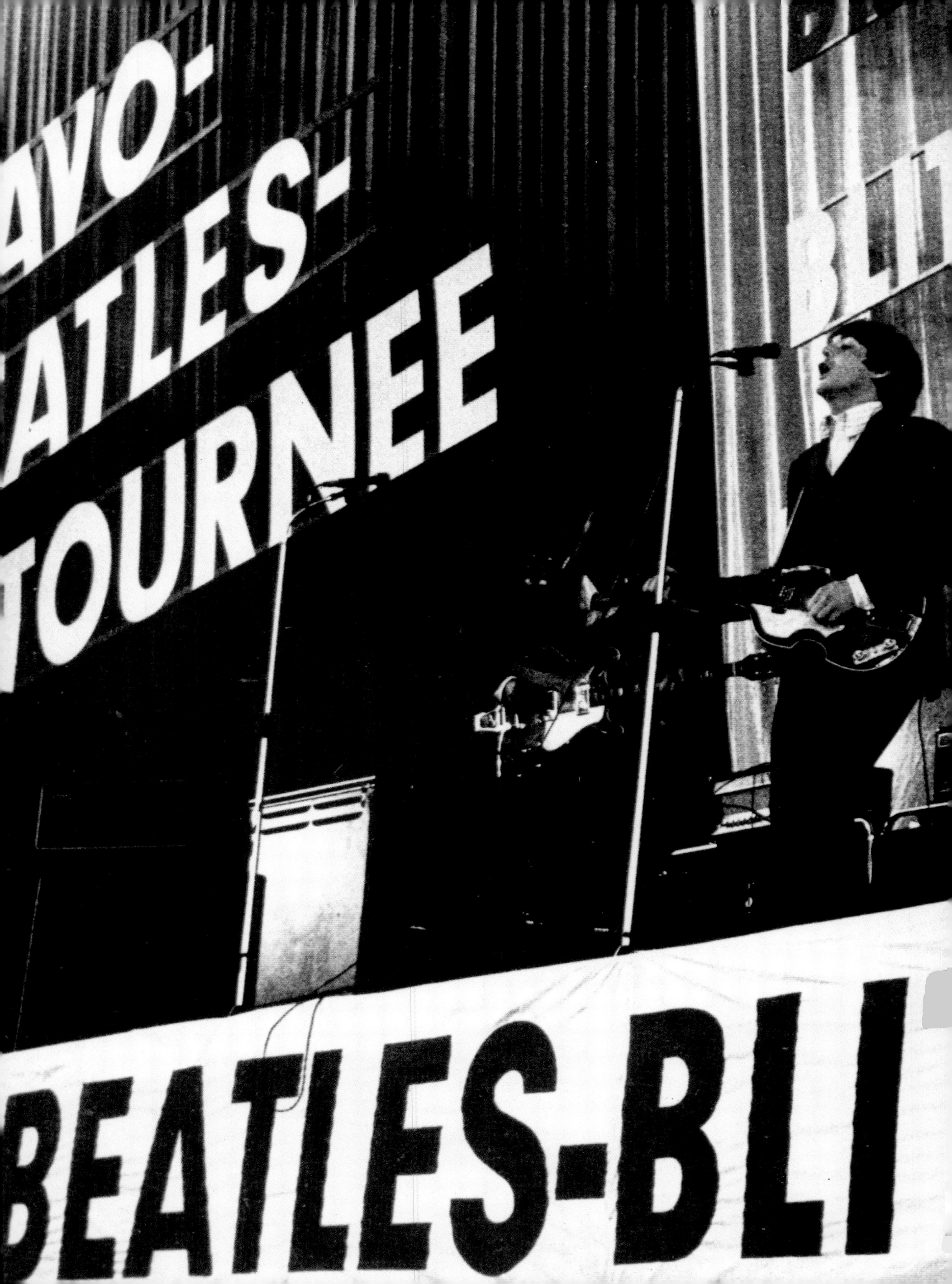
AVO-
ATLES-
TOURNEE
BLI
BEATLES-BLI

"Martin Sharp added the caption later. Someone had come up to John at the Ad Lib Club and said 'If you've got a spare minute, could you write me a song?'"

George, Brian and John resting after the concert at Essen, June 1966.

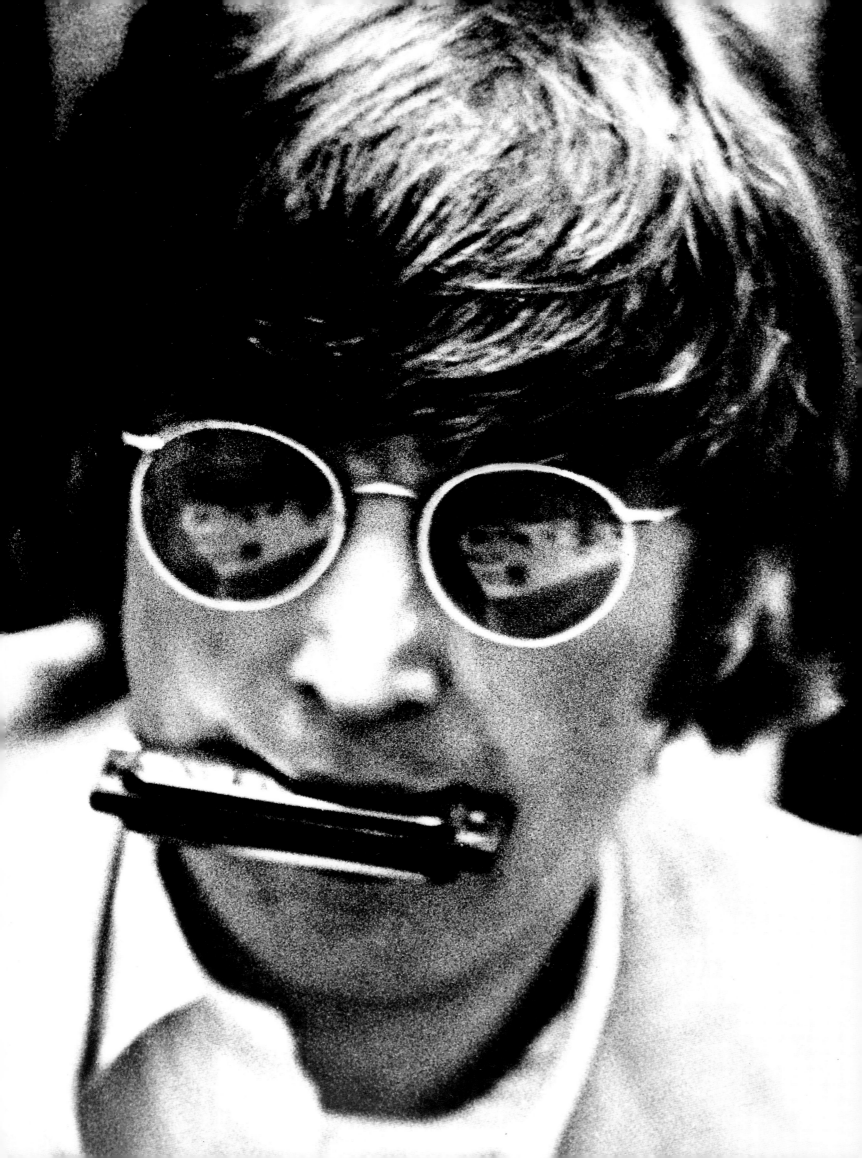

"This was on a train between Essen and Hamburg. We were told the coach had been Hitler's, and had later been used by the Queen. John was constantly reading on tour, and here he shares a joke from a Thurber book with Brian."

John and Brian en route to Hamburg, June 1966.

A fleeting glimpse of John in a moment of great enthusiasm, Munich, June 1966.

Overleaf: John and Brian, Munich, June 1966.

ON TOUR: JAPAN

John on the plane to Tokyo, June 1966.

From Germany, Bob flew with the Beatles to Tokyo for the group's one and only series of concerts in Japan. En route they stopped briefly in London to change planes, and there was an unscheduled break at Anchorage, Alaska, to avoid a typhoon. It would be the Beatles' penultimate tour, and the last one on which Bob accompanied them. An era was coming to an end.

Bob's photographs leading up to, and during, the concerts at the Nippon Budokan Hall in Tokyo brilliantly encapsulate the pace and excitement of a Beatles gig, and highlight the expectation and hysteria their performances generated.

Between performances, the Beatles were incarcerated for three days and nights, for their own safety, in their suite at the Tokyo Hilton. They were anxious to take back souvenirs of Japan and all manner of tradesmen were shown into their rooms with objects for the Beatles to buy. While confined there they embarked on a unique collaboration. They ordered up paints and brushes, each took a corner of a large sheet of Japanese hand-made paper, and together they worked on a four-man painting.

As they painted, the acetate of *Revolver* played constantly; they listened and sang along to it, deciding on the final positioning of the tracks on the album, which was released six weeks later.

Overleaf: Jetlagged on arrival at Tokyo, June 1966.

John in the hotel, Tokyo, June 1966.

Following pages:
Run-up to the Budokan concert, July 1966.

Driving to the Nippon Budokan, Tokyo, July 1966.

The Beatles taking the stage at the Budokan, Tokyo, July 1966.

The Budokan concerts,
Tokyo, July 1966.

John and Japanese mask, Tokyo Hilton, July 1966.

"The Beatles were genuinely interested in what Japan had to offer.
They bought kites, gold lacquer boxes, ivory miniatures and netsuke from
the traders. John was particularly fascinated by the Japanese masks."

George, Brian and John,
Tokyo, July 1966.

Room 1005 – The Presidential Suite. The group painting in the
Tokyo Hilton, June/July 1966.

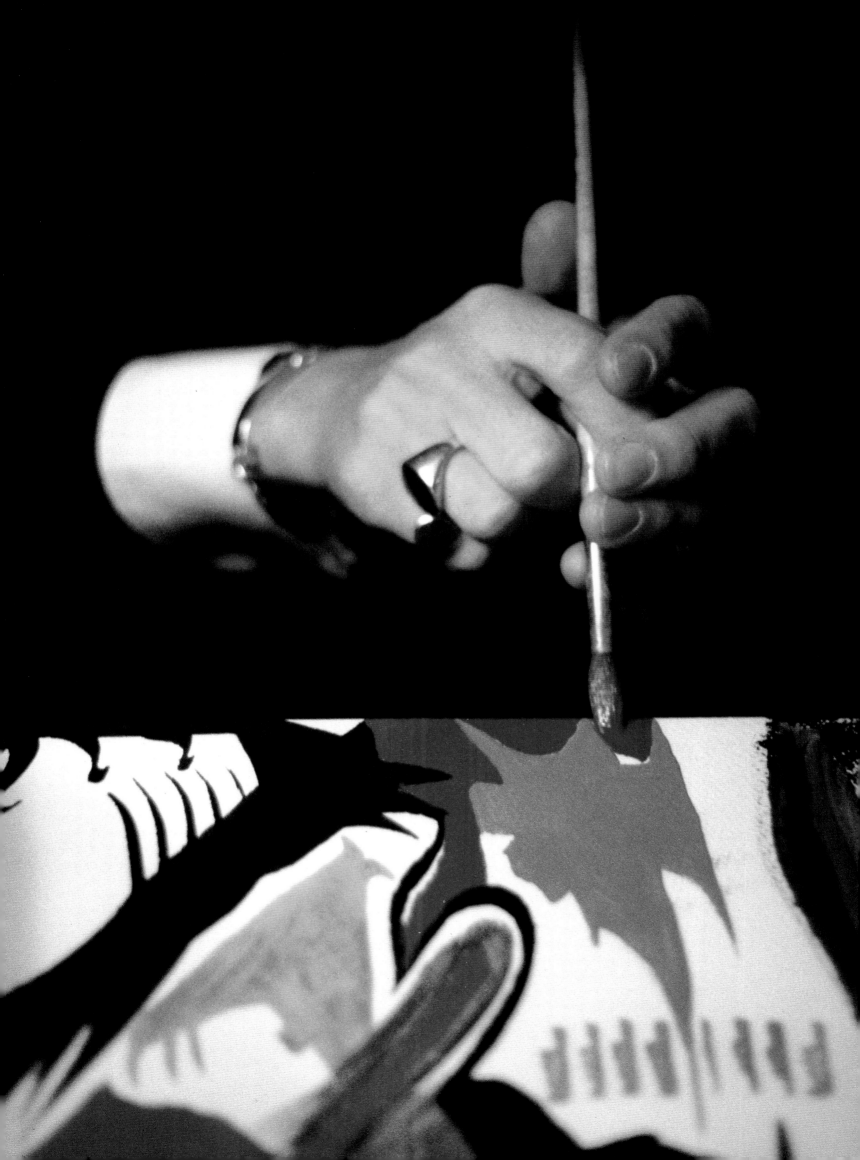

"Other than their music this painting was the only creative
enterprise I saw the Beatles undertake as a group. I had
never seen them so happy – no drink, no drugs, no girls –
just working together with no distractions."

John defacing a Beatles portrait. Flying from Tokyo to Manila, July 1966.

Overleaf: Stopover in Hong Kong, July 1966.

John interviewed in Hong Kong, July 1966.

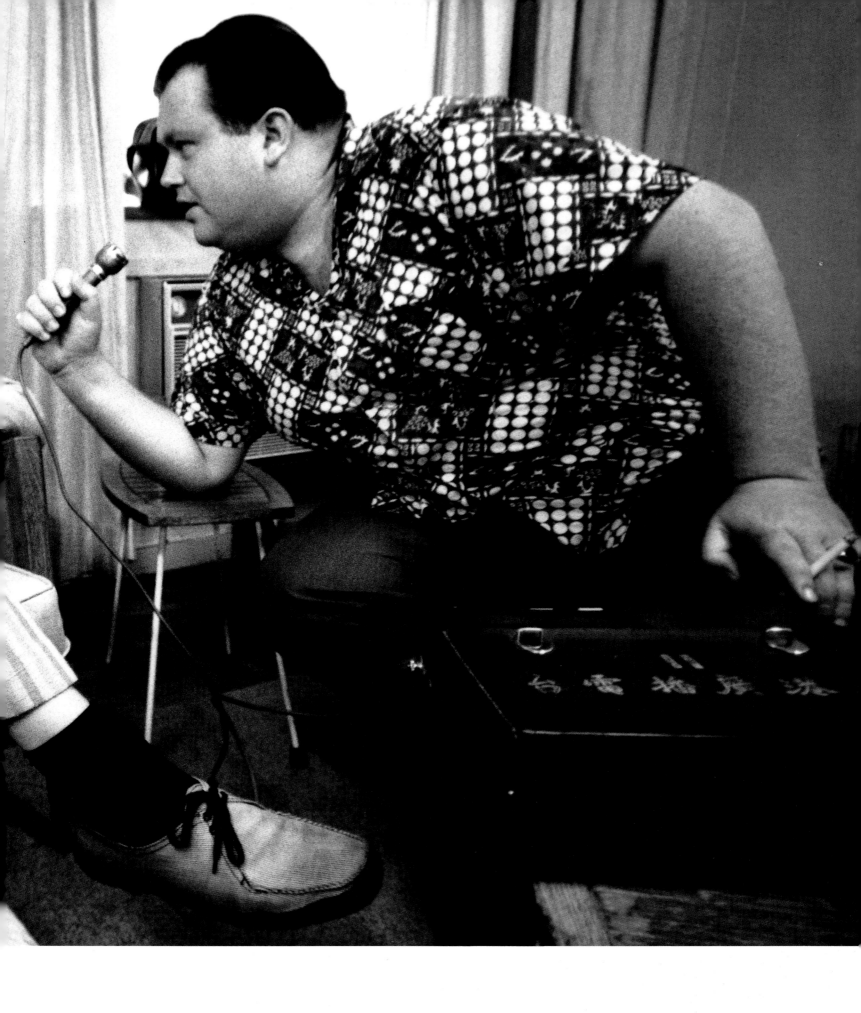

Overleaf: Preparing to leave Hong Kong airport, July 1966.

EAST OF ESHER

WELL IT'S CERTAINLY NOT TOBACCO

On August 29 1966 the Beatles gave their last ever public performance in San Francisco. They continued to work together in the studio until the end of the sixties, but the final concert marked the beginning of the break-up of the Beatles. They pursued individual projects, asserting their creative independence from one another, none more so than George. Two weeks after returning from the U.S. tour, George and his wife Patti flew to India to study yoga and the sitar.

When the Beatles ceased touring, so, inevitably, came the end of Bob's association with NEMS Enterprises. The split was natural and amicable; as they all went their separate ways Bob undertook one last project, photographing the transformation of the Harrisons' bungalow in Esher. It was a crossroads in all their careers. George had been the first Beatle to embrace Eastern music and mysticism, and on his return from India he repainted his Surrey home in a naïve psychedelic manner. Part Bombay and part Haight-Ashbury, its amorphous style recalls the Beatles' slightly earlier joint painting venture in Tokyo.

In contrast to George's do-it-yourself aesthetic the more professionally-painted fireplace at Esher was the work of Dutch artists Marijke Koger and Simon Postuma. They were members of a hippy group called 'The Fool' who were best known for their eclectic mural on the Beatles' Apple boutique in London's Baker Street. Opened in December 1967, the shop marked the end of the year that had seen the release of *Sergeant Pepper* and the death of Brian Epstein – the old Beatles order had changed for ever.

George painting the house at Esher, October 1966.

Patti Harrison in the garden at Esher, October 1966.

Kinfauns goes psychedelic, Esher, October 1966.

Bob found a prism lying on George's coffee table. He decided to place
it in front of his lens and photograph Marijke and George through it.
The multiple-image that resulted had a hallucinatory quality
that would become very popular on psychedelic album covers.

George through a prism, Esher, October 1966.

Marijke Koger, Esher, October 1966.

The fireplace at Esher, painted by Marijke Koger, October 1966.

MYTHS AND METAPHYSICS

"Nothing is solid, everything is an illusion."

Photographing on tour, Bob had intimate access to the private Beatles. He was never required to use artificial lighting in order to provide standard-issue 'clean' publicity pictures. Instead, he was free to record events in a way which, if sometimes short on straightforward Beatle information, was very strong on atmosphere. Nevertheless, these dramatic photo-reportages were different in character from the photographs which he had been making in Australia, and which had made such an impression on Brian Epstein.

All this changed in April 1965 when Bob visited John and Cynthia Lennon at their house in Weybridge. The Beatles' earliest photographers were specialists in tame studio shots or patronizing, fooling around mop-top pictures. Though the situation improved with Robert Freeman's graphic cover for their *With the Beatles* album at the end of 1963, things happened too fast in the years of Beatlemania to allow a coherent policy towards Beatle visuals to be formulated. But it is clear that Brian Epstein had recognized in Bob Whitaker someone with an individual approach that paralleled the Beatles' own growing rejection of pop conventions, and whose work might reflect the group's own changing ideas.

In this respect Bob's photographs of the Lennons represent a remarkable turning point. Never before had anyone broken away so determinedly from the accepted mould of Beatle photography. The series completely turns around any notion of promoting the Beatles. It shows John and Cynthia collaborating in a project of Bob's devising, and underlines the trust they were willing to place in his personal view of the Beatles phenomenon.

Because Narcissus did not return the love of the nymph Echo, Venus caused him to become enamoured of his own reflection in the waters of a fountain. He pined away until he was changed into a flower. Nobody ever accused John of personal vanity, but on another level this was an astonishingly prophetic photograph.

Cynthia looks on as John plays Narcissus in the garden of their Weybridge home, May 1965.

"John and I never discussed the Beatles. He was interested in metaphysics and art, and in particular we talked about the act of creating a work of art."

John and Cynthia, Weybridge, March 1965.

John with flower,
Weybridge, May 1965.

To Dear old Bob.
a friend indeed
with whom I have spent
many happy hours in
fruitful discussion.
long life and
health
to you old buddy
from John

P.S. Piss off yer
owld bastard!

John's second book of writings, *A Spaniard in the Works*,
was published in 1965 and he duly inscribed a copy,
in his inimitable style, to Bob.

John and Cynthia, Weybridge, May 1965.

The composition of this photograph was not, as one might have expected, indebted to Grant Wood's famous painting *American Gothic*, which Bob did not know at the time. In fact the idea was based on a photograph he had made of Nigel Buesst and his girlfriend back in Melbourne in 1963. Trying to re-create the appearance of early Australian photographs of the 1860s, he had posed his friends in the manner of pioneering settlers, in front of a colonial weatherboarded house He pictured the Lennons in a similar way, not as part of the Beatles myth but as a happy hard-working family, doing their best to earn a living. The large gold spoon clutched by Julian Lennon brings a more realistic note to Bob's own fantasy.

The Lennon family, Weybridge, May 1965.

This session in a Chelsea studio also resulted in the Beatles'
participation in a bizarre project which Bob called a
"Somnambulant Adventure". Originally he had planned the
series as a triptych, along the lines of a religious icon. It was to
be his personal comment on the mass adulation of the group and
the illusory nature of stardom. The sequence begins with the
'birth' of the Beatles, a string of sausages doing service as the
umbilical cord. George hammers nails into John's head to
emphasize that even Beatles are flesh and blood like anyone else.
The complete series was never published, although the final
image was used on the cover of *The Beatles Yesterday and
Today* album in the U.S. It showed the mirthful Beatles
surrounded by slabs of red meat and dismembered dolls – way
out of line with their public image. Out of context, the photograph
shocked many fans. It was soon withdrawn, and had to be quickly
replaced by a conventional studio shot of four rather bored
Beatles. But as John later pointed out, less squeamish buyers soon
discovered that you could steam off the replacement and get
back to the original.

And your bird can sing. Martin Sharp's over-drawing of a flower
recalls Surrealist André Masson's famous 1938 painting *Girl in a
Black Gag With a Pansy Mouth*. In fact Bob was looking for a way
to symbolize "that these two guys had beautiful singing voices —
they literally sang like canaries".

John and Ringo, London, March 1966.

George and John, London, March 1966.

"I wanted to illustrate the idea that, in a way, there was nothing more amazing about Ringo than anyone else on this earth. In this life he was just one of two million members of the human race. The idolization of fans reminded me of the story of the worship of the golden calf."

From the *Yesterday and Today* session,
London, March 1966.

In an interview just two months before he
was murdered in 1980, John Lennon
explained how these photographs came
about. Bob, he recalled ". . . was into Dali
and making Surreal pictures . . . It was
inspired by our boredom and resentment
at having to do *another* photo session and
another Beatles thing. We were sick to
death of it . . . That combination produced
that cover."

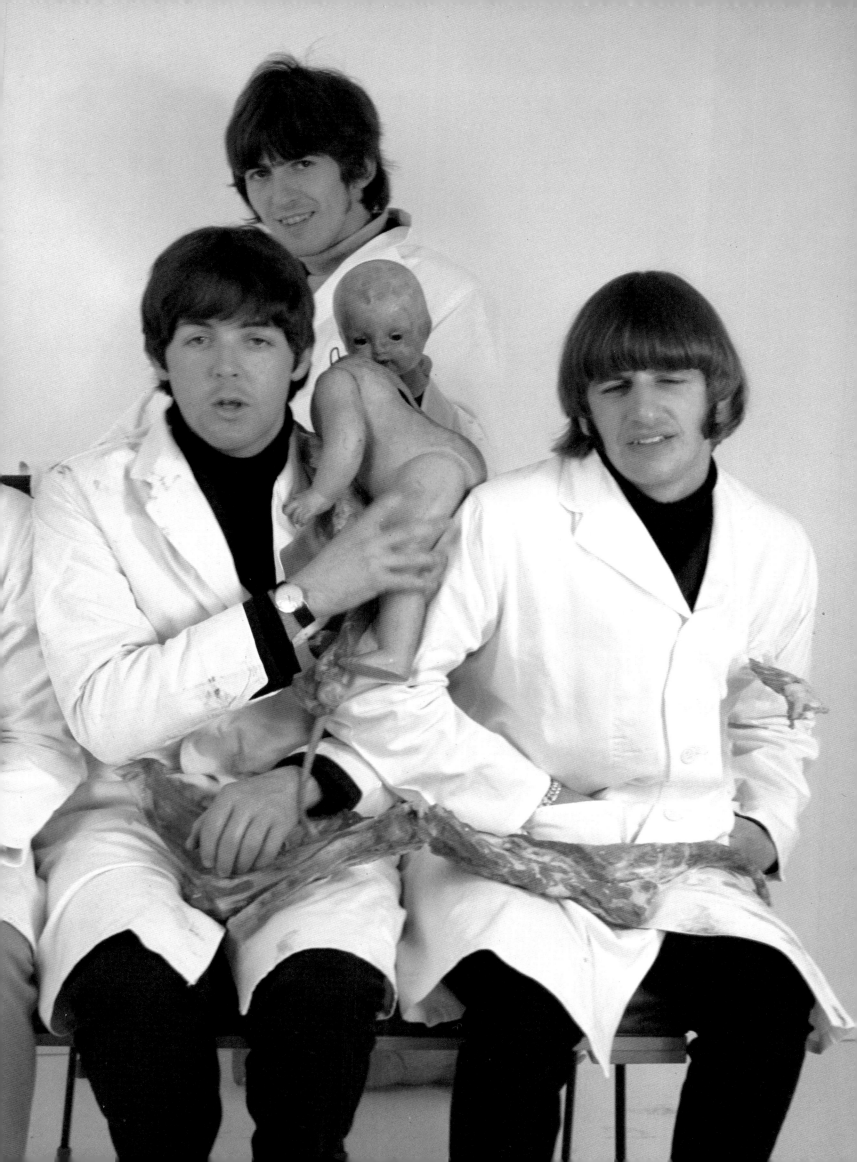

150

AFTER THE BREAK

Towards the end of 1966 Bob found an ideal studio/apartment at the legendary Pheasantry Studios complex on London's King's Road. He was joined there by an old friend, Martin Sharp, recently arrived from Australia. Earlier in the sixties Sharp had been associated with Richard Neville in an early incarnation of *Oz* as a satirical magazine back in Australia. Now, with Sharp as graphic designer and Bob Whitaker as photographer, Neville was re-launching the title as the London underground's monthly. The first issue was published in February 1967, and although Bob only stayed for five months it was long enough to see the magazine become established as a famous – or infamous – addition to the underground press.

In the months leading up to *Oz* both Bob's photographic career and Martin's attempts to find employment as a cartoonist were meet-ing with limited success. With time on their hands they worked at several joint projects. They re-cycled some of Bob's Beatle photographs as poster ideas and humorous cartoons, though none were published. Their most ambitious and compelling scheme was for a Beatles calendar. This too, until today, has never seen the light of day. Indeed it was never completed, though only, recalls Bob, ''. . . because we gave up after spilling a bottle of Indian ink over one of the pictures''.

Martin Sharp went on to gain justified acclaim for his psychedelic posters and album covers. For one of these, Cream's *Disraeli Gears* (November 1967), Bob supplied the portraits of the group for the dayglo montage. Bob's career in photography successfully expanded into many different areas, but this was his last brush with the world of pop music.

APRIL   FOOL

FRIDAY   SATURDAY   SUNDAY   MONDAY   TUESDAY   THURSD   THURSDAY

1 2 3 4 5 6 7

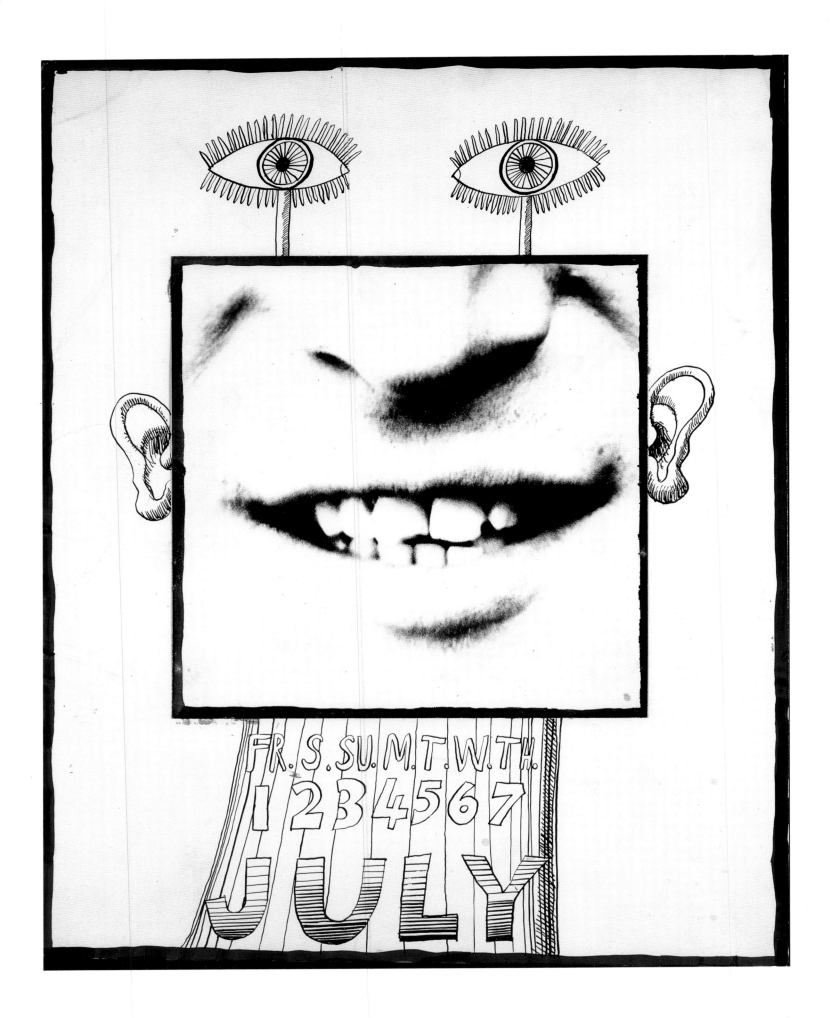

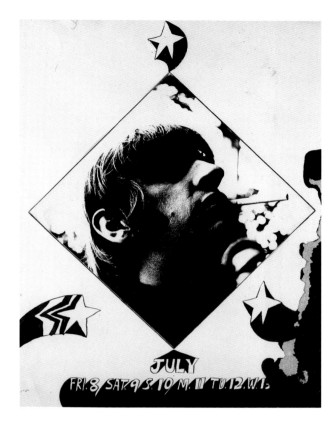

In June 1965 each of the Beatles was awarded the M.B.E.
Later, John revealed that they had smoked pot
in the Buckingham Palace toilets
while waiting for the Queen to present their honours.
Martin Sharp's collage is a witty reference to this,
but also reminds us that John, in particular, was far from
unequivocal about having accepted the award.